For Julian and for Roman

Thomas Allosaurus looked like a Tyrannosaurus. He was big and he was loud and the leaves fell from the trees when he walked around.

He might have looked mean, but he wouldn't hurt a bean. And Thomas had a problem, see, his teeth weren't clean!

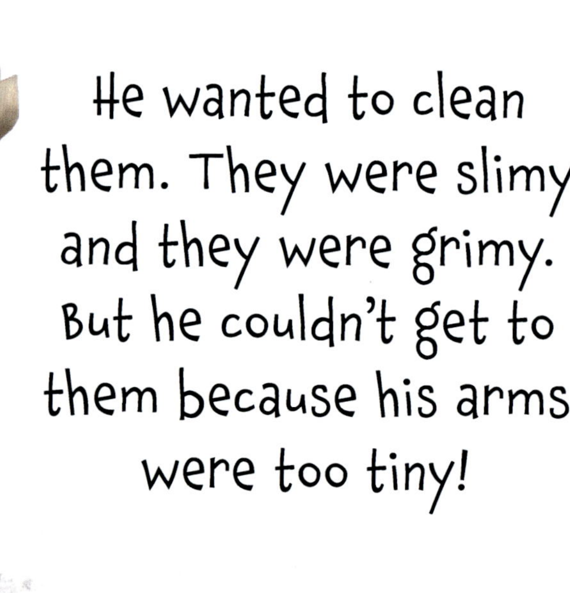

He wanted to clean them. They were slimy and they were grimy. But he couldn't get to them because his arms were too tiny!

If someone could help him, he would be so much happier. But no one came near him. They were scared he would eat them!

Then out popped a mouse from his tiny little house. His name was Paul and he wasn't afraid of Thomas at all.

Thomas said, "Hello there, friend. I've got a few problems. They're inside my mouth. Do you think you can solve them?"

Paul said, “Let me guess. You can’t brush your teeth because your arms can’t reach. Well I bet I can reach if I use a big leaf.”

Paul got a big leaf and he rubbed on the teeth, but they weren't getting clean so he stopped to think.

Maybe some sticks would work better he figured. So he ran for a while and he scooped up a pile.

He rubbed the stick pile on Thomas' smile, but it still wouldn't get clean, so again, he stopped to think.

Paul said, “You know, I rub my teeth on my fur. It sounds kind of weird but it works for sure.”

Thomas said, “But I have no fur. What can I do to bring my mouth back to health?”

Paul said, “I have an idea. I can just use myself!”

Paul got in position and he scrubbed with some friction. He went in between and around. He was a mouse on a mission.

He scrubbed the front teeth and the back teeth and the middle teeth and the little teeth.

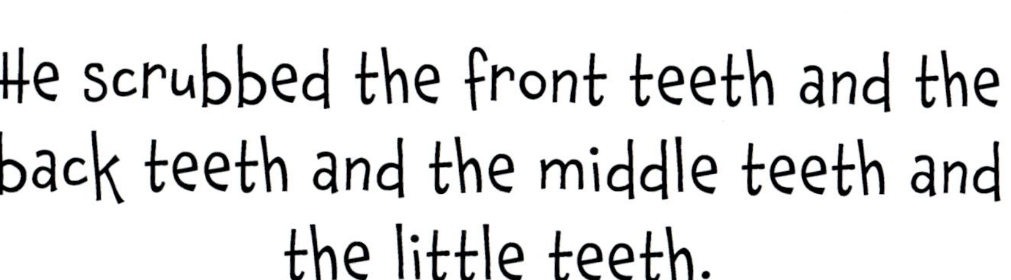

"How does it look?" Thomas asked with a grin.
"I can see my reflection," Paul said. "I'd call it perfection."

Thomas said, "Thank you, friend. Now I
can stand tall. But look at you now. You're a
grimy fuzzball!"

“Why help an Allosaurus who looks very scary? Even when doing so makes you grimy, and very.”

"Being an Allosaurus doesn't mean that you're scary," Paul said. "Being scary makes you scary, and you've been nothing but friendly."

"I'm glad you came along and helped me," Thomas said. "Now that we're friends, let's do something fun!"

"Sure," Paul said. "But first I'll need a bath, a really long one."

Made in the USA
Middletown, DE
25 October 2021